POEMS FROM THE HEART

by

Margaret Upson

Also by Margaret Upson

Easy To Read
Easy To Read II
Poems For A Special Friend - ISBN 1 902869 02 8

Published & Printed by Just Print IT! Publications
59 The Whaddons, Huntingdon, Cambs. PE29 1NW
Tel: 01480 450880

ISBN 1 902869 12 5

First Edition

POEMS FROM THE HEART

was born in Titchmarsh, Northants and began writing poetry in 1995. Anchor Books, Poets-Now and Triumph House have also published some of my poems.

My friends and family encourage me to write my poems and all my royalties I give to charities, mainly helping children with disabilities to have a little better life.

To my
Friends, family and all my readers,
without whom there would be no poems.

Margaret Upson 2000

To My Dear Cousin Sandra.
X Best Wishes X
Margaret Upson
25 June 2000.

IN STYLE

We celebrated the new century in style
As the bells rang we rested awhile
Joining in the millennium break
There was a film they tried to make

Moments reflecting with love ones near
And the memories we hold so clear
It made us much more aware of time
And being a new year when the last bells chime

The collection we all can share
Like the fun we had at the village fair
The sky was lit up like the northern lights
Every one was there, even little mites

Barbecues with everything to eat
For the children a special treat
Even the rain stayed away
A lovely night for a special day

Slowly people wonder home
Even the ones visiting the Dome
And we pray the world will be at peace
Loving our neighbours and being at ease

THE PASSING YEARS

Rooms where not heated when we were small
The beds where put against the wall
You always looked so forlorn
You put your feet on me to get them warm

Our light was a small wax candle
Stood in a stick with a small handle
We had to clean and re-light the fire
With a brush it's bristles made from wire

From the yard we fetched wood and coal
Empty hot water into a large bowl
Did not take long to warm the cruel
Bellies filled we went off to school

No such thing as a car or bus
We never even made a fuss
As we went we'd play and sing
Our food for school we did bring

Our prayers we always had to say
Thanking the Lord for our work and play
Times where hard, but often good
Those years were the past, they done what they could

NEVER BE AFRAID

Our Lord keeps watch on me though the night
Helps me to be healthy and bright
He's always by my side
And always my loving guide
He gives me a sign to slow down
And not to act too much the clown
Helps with the poems I write
Helps me to see the light
If you ask him he'll help you too
In all you say and what you do
So when you sit or kneel to pray
Ask for his blessing from day to day
We our souls he does keep
He's there if we're awake or asleep
There's a lot we should thank God for
He always has an open door
You can easily enter his garden gate
He is our destiny, guide and fate
Thank you Lord for helping me
And for the good things I do and see
Thank you for my good faithful friend
Someone to love to my end

LIGHT OF WAY

For His love we don't have to beg
He's a faithful friend, and by your side
He sends the sun to keep us warm
To clear the air sends a storm
To purify the earth He sends frost and snow
All of which makes everything grow
When things go from worst to bad
We get low, depressed and sad
Suddenly we have a open mind
Everything is better so we find
You never see Him come with in
He helps all, even if you sin
He'll always understands
Always there to hold your hand
He will guide us every day
If we ask when we pray

TENDERNESS

Your the man with the key to my heart
And it's getting harder to be a part
Everyday I wait for him to come at last
He says don't worry the waiting days will pass
I recall our first lovely meeting
My silly heart nearly stopped beating
And what a lovely day we had
When he left me I was sad
He was caring, full of tenderness
He help me overcome my loneliness
When we parted he held me tight
We kissed and said goodnight
Whilst talking he said he would phone
That way I would not be on my own

SHADOWS

To see the shadows large and small
Watching them grow then fall
A shadow of a bird on the ground
Looking for food that can be found
And of things in the town
Of the leaves as they tumble down
The best shadows are in the morn
They come in with the dawn
Of the night life we hardly see
As the day starts to break they flee
Mainly caused by the sun
Who rises to get all things done
There's even shadows as we sleep
From the moon as across the sky he'll creep
None of these will do us harm
It's all a part of our earth's charm

SEARCHING

Snow laying thickly on the ground
Birds searching for food that can be found
Children building things from the snow
Toes, finger cold, and noses aglow
Down the hill they will slide
Over the ice on a sleigh they glide
Weathering another snow storm
Wrapped up to keep themselves warm
Pine logs heat up the sitting room
Curtains closed to keep out the gloom
But not everyone has any heat
No warm shoes on their feet
Some around the country still roam
As they have no work or a home
The church evening service will soon begin
For a little warmth they can sit within

DAYS OF OLD

In Victorians days people were stricken and poor
Even children scrubbed steps and a stone floor
No such thing as a vacuum sweep
For this job boys they would keep
Climbing inside amongst the fumes and smoke
It's a wonder on the soot some didn't choke

Orphans were treated rough and cruel
Fed on dry bread and watered gruel
School days some never had
To get away some where glad
Many lads went of to sea
In fresh air they hoped to be

A few worked in the stables with a groom
Sharing a bed in a attic room
Girls worked from the corner of the street
Poorly clothed no shoes on their feet
When we think we've got it bad
Remember the hard times those families had

WHY

Why can't we ever learn
Why on others do we turn
Why is there so much abuse
Why make a fuss at what we choose

Why can't more people be a friend
Why must there be bitter ends
Why do children always suffer
Why not make life less rougher

Why don't teenagers try to behave
Why don't we all turn over the page
Why do we have to have war
Why in life people make flaws

Why don't we learn how to pray
Just listen, and try to obey
Why not read the good book
And at ourselves take a good look

BEING A JERK

I've got lonelier since my pal past away
But the memories of her are here to stay
Every day she would always phone
To see if I was alright as I lived alone
Now I read and write for hours
even by myself some flowers
Several years our friendship did not part
carry it all now in my heart
To visit her grave can never be
As there is not one for anyone to see
She left us all without a goodbye
To find another friend, I'm to old to try
Now she'd say I was being a jerk
Guess I better get on with some work

LITTLE OLD LADY

Just a little old lady of working class
In her youth a lively lass
Every morning you can see
Taking her dog for a spree

She'd always give a neighbour a hand
Doing gardening, or mixing cement and sand
Even worked in Godmanchester mill
Sad to say the mill is now still

Walked to Houghton every day
Washing, cleaning , and little pay
In a factory she made jam
Those days we could not afford ham

She even did a daily paper round
In all weathers she could be found
She's not afraid of working hard
Some remember her and send a card

Never sick or on the dole
We know her as Lou ,a happy soul
Skip she got from Woodgreen
She cares for him and keeps him clean

On the bus he loves to ride
Near her feet, or by her side
Lou would give her last penny
If someone she knew had not any

RHYME AND LAUGH

We've all heard of little boy blue
And the old lady in a shoe
Little Bo Peep sold her sheep
The boy in the haystack washed his feet
Pussy got a drink from the well
Jack and Jill were drunk when they fell

Around the clock a wee mouse ran
While Simple Simon done the cancan
Blackbirds ate the crusty pie
When Georgy Porgie made the girls cry
Humpty Dumpty was a fool
With Mary's lamb they played truant from school

Mother goose made us learn
We should not speak out of turn
If the sheep we could not count
So the old dame gave us a clout
Now all back into the shoe
A slice of bread and no stew

COLD NIGHT

It was a cold and bitter night
The great north star was shining bright
The moon was only half way round
Cats were fighting for scrapes they found
Carol singers in the street
Some had warm shoes on their feet
As they went from door to door
Collecting so they could help the poor
The soup kitchen was open Xmas night
The hall door was lit with a bright light
They needed hot food that Xmas day
For the homeless that came their way
Some had a small gift
From what was left
In some places they had a bed
A hot drink, cheese and some bread
Daytime they would beg for more
Even a dog gave us his paw
A lady gave him a bone
Said she'd hate Xmas alone
To beg must hurt within
There must be some where they can stay in

A NANNA'S SMILE

A little girl knelt by her Nanna's chair
A lot of things they did often share
A lot the girl did not understand
So gently she took her Nanna's hand

Nan why do you always smile
Don't you get lonely once in awhile
Because dear child you bring me joy
Just like your father when he was a boy

Seeing you playing happily on the lawn
I may get lonely ,but not forlorn
Many is the hour I watch you play
Your my sunshine come what may

Your tears only come when you fall
I'm always here when you call
The smile on my face is what you bring
In your laughter and when you sing

The smile comes from the heart
It's always there to play it's part
A smile of joy, the happiness I'll always show
For the loveliest little girl I know

THE PHOTOGRAPH

She gazed at the photograph she'd had for years
She'd had so much hardship and many tears
How often had she 'd been down memory lane
Still the heart break would remain
Remembering how he walked out the door
Shouting he was feed up being poor
For years for him she did yearn
But not once did he ever return
She never guest he'd signed up for the war
Just like his father had done before
So many men, boys went that day
Some into the army volunteered to stay
They thought they had a chance
But a lot was sent over to France
The day they thought they would save
They were honest men and very brave
But it was not the way to get rich
Fighting and hiding in a ditch
Through the war some came back
But of him she'd lost track
But now as she was growing old
The true story in her memory she now told

TO LEARN THE TRUTH

Do we believe all we are told
At the end of a rainbow there is gold
Watch our children come to no harm
Never panic always calm
Go to church to Our Lord pray
Or put it off for another day

From the bad land Moses led the way
And to the mountains he went to pray
The Lord gave him the commandments, his law
The people with Moses did not want a war
God's teaching and work we all know
But that's as far as some of us go

But I've a friend who became a reader
Through him I became a true believer
The goodness of his heart we can reach
Only the truth is what he'll preach
Every sermon a lesson he will tell
The people know him and trust him as well

OUR SPECIAL LADY

The Christmas story went as planned
Everyone was there to lend a hand
A lady as Mary played her part
Pulled the strings of every ones heart
The inn keeper look so forlorn
He had no room for the babe to be born
They found a stable the bible said
And the manger became the babies bed
An angel appeared to the shepherds and he did say
Fear not, Mary's boy child was born today
As the shepherds to the stable drew near
In their eyes they showed a tear
Three wise men travelled far
Guided by a big bright star
The carpenter Joseph had a dream
The angel came and told him what it did mean
He said take your family away today
As the wicked king, the babe he would slay
So to Egypt they did go to dwell
The Christmas story people still tell
We celebrate the birth of the special baby
And the love and courage of Joseph and Our Lady

HE LOVES US

Jesus loves his children large and small
He will always answer when we call
For what we do, with money he does not pay
All He gives us is to share ,not throw away
When we think all is lost
Think of Him who died on the cross
He died to save us all, and will rise again
Not for nothing did He go through the pain
Oh there are times we remember
Like the twenty fifth of December
But there are other times to recalled
When wars cause people to fall
So to Our Lord we should pray
Ask Him to guide us every night and day
And in illness teach us to be brave
And from the war people save
To help each other as long as we live
And our enemies help and try to forgive

SPRING BEAUTY

Violets hide in the shade
Primroses cover a leafy glade
Mauves, white and the deepest blue
Shows just where the bluebells are peeping through

As we listen to the whispering breeze
We can see bursting buds in the trees
Fox gloves shake their pretty heads
Green ferns make fawns lovely beds

Everywhere is a picture of beauty
Nature has certainly done her duty
A lot of flowers can be seen
And colours of every shade of green

LITTLE LADY

Lovely soft brown velvet eyes
Taking people by surprise
You don't look like a English rose
Dark hair and a turned up nose
Neither do you come from the emerald isle
Not with that love, wistful smile

There seems to be no beauty you lack
For some reason you love to dress in black
Of yourself you seem to be sure
But of you there's a lot more
On a pony you love to ride
On your skates you love to glide

In the water you love to swim
I don't know where to begin
A trip to France has been planned
And a visit to wonderful Disney land
Photographs, memories to keep and care
With your family you can always share

IF ONLY

IF only things went as we planned
IF only you were here to hold my hand
IF only we could see the future
IF only we did not grow to mature

IF only life could be rearranged
IF only things we could change
IF only into our heart we could look
IF only we all saw the risks we took

IF only I could see you a lot more
IF only you'd walk though my door
IF only you'd keep the promises you made
IF only memories would not fade

IF only I new which path to take
IF only I would not make a mistake
IF only these wars would come to an end
IF only on each other we could depend

THE SHEPHERD

At night while the valley was asleep
An old shepherd would watch his sheep
Where they were he could always tell
He listen to the tinkle of their bell
His faithful friend goes around the flock
Keeping guard of the stock

She found a orphan lamb alone
The shepherd would find it a home
Although the valley was clear that night
The snow could come when it was light
Close to his chalet he had stacks of hay
Beds for his sheep and lambs to lay

To keep them from harm and the cold
He'd bring them into his warm fold
When his wife went it broke his heart
His lovely animals and chalet he'd never part
The valley and people gave him a reason
To be happy and love every season

WE HAVE CHANGED

First thing in the morning the cock will crow
Come every body it's time to get up and go
Dad gets his water from the barrel to wash
Hot or cold if it's frozen the ice he'll crush
We did not have a shower ,just a tin bath
Placed in front of the fire by the hearth
Clean out the ashes, sieve and put away
To light the boiler outside on wash day
No cereal to have we had jam and bread
We never went hungry there was dripping instead
There were no fridge's or freezers to keep things in
Everything fresh, bottled not even a tin
Fresh veg, fruit was stored ,bottled or made into jam
At Xmas and Sundays, we'd have home cured bacon or ham
No gas or electric all done on a range
Now over the years all that had to change
Diesel and electric trains took over the steam engine
Tractors now toil the land, harvest reaped by a combine
Everything is canned or frozen for us to buy
No lovely suet puddings or country pie
All old things have vanished or been put in a show
And everything is still changing this we know

HE FOUND THE BEST

The hunger pains began to gnaw
His feet were cold and very sore
In some straw he fell asleep
There was a dream he'd like to keep

To London he had come alone
Now he wished he had been home
Gradually things were getting bad
He'd spent everything he had

The nights were getting cold
The streets were not paved with gold
That night he would dream of the sea
And the heavenly place where it would be

And the captain would be his friend
But he never lived to see the end
On a heavenly boat he found the best
And in God's arms he found his rest

NEVER DULL

Maybe I should ride my bike
In fine weather take a hike
No good taking out the car
Cause I'm not going that far
I did try a slow jog
Got overtaken by a road hog
As he passed he nearly had us over
With muddy water he did us cover
Along the road there is no path
To see us jump made him laugh
The wind and lorry have a pull
Life on the road is never dull

WHERE I REST

I wish like a bird I could fly
Soaring up into the blue sky
Swooping down like a peregrine
Speeding through the air on a wing

I wish I could get a birds eye view
Seeing things as they often do
Watch out for trouble on the land
That would really be grand

A bird can sit on a tree to rest
And if it's safe they'll build a nest
Hiding away from predators who keep watch
To see the eggs when they hatch

Well in a plane I can fly
Watching all views as we go by
But I could never build a nest
I have a home in which to rest

DAY DREAMER

I often go down to the stream
Sit by the water and day dream
We use to go on a boat for a tanner
Now a few years later cost a Tenner

In the stream, I watch the chub
Searching around for some grub
The water seems so very shallow
I dreamt I left it for tomorrow

From that daydream I woke up with a start
I suddenly realise where I was at
As I got up a boat was mooring
Thundering and it was pouring

In my dream it did not rain
Now I'm awake and soaked again
I had no umbrella nor a hat
But it was sunny when on the bank I sat

BED TIME STORY

At night is when I sit and think
Leaving the dishes in the sink
But it's not time to go to bed
And three times that book I've read

I had a pie, peas and mash for tea
And that was plenty for me
Well might as well run my bath
Put my slippers near the hearth

I'm not very big or bold
I hate it when my feet are cold
Once I've had a good old scrub
By the fire I'll give my back a rub

Cold weather, of a good fire I'm glad
Life with out it could be sad
So now a hot drink I'm of to bed
There's nothing to do, nowt to be said

VERY RELUCTANT TO GO

Very reluctant to leave his mother alone
He never planned to leave his home
He was a young man who had to enlist
From the mill, he walked though the sea mist
The pain on his mother's face he saw
He lost two brothers and father in the war
Know one seemed to bother or understand
To go into the forces he had not planned
He had a good job for the start
He hated breaking his mother's heart
The old mill stood very proud
It's little tea room brought in the crowd
He would have to do the best he can
At eighteen he was classed as a man
He knew it was only for two years
As he walked away he shed a few tears
Men they say should never cry
Why not to want to go would be a lie
The mill he kept in good repair
His home with his mother he did share
On her own his mother would stay
For the two long years he was away

THEY WAKE WITH THE DAWN

As the night turns into the dawn
We start a bright new morn
The blackbird is the first to wake
On the breeze his song will break

Then comes the gentle dove
Telling his song of love
Crows take to the air
Warning all to be aware

Other birds sing listen to me
Some in the hedges or up a tree
But the cockerel won't be beat
To his hens he is discreet

From the wood a pigeon will coo
And an old owl says it's to wet to woo
A woodpecker search the tree bark
There's a lovely song from a lark

In the day a nightingale will sing
Lot's of different songs a joy they bring
Who wants TV, disco or a radio
The dawn chorus has a long way to go

SUNBEAMS

Open your curtains let me though
You'll feel better if you do
I'll put a smile on your face
Cure those tears without a trace

Through the trees my sunbeams dance
And though your windows if they get a chance
I come over the wall, or round the back
My sunbeams never return or go slack

I'll warm the coldest day and night
Warm the earth and keep it bright
Help to make most things grow
Melt the ice, thaw the snow

I also bring in the light
Make things beautiful and bright
Try to keep the dark clouds away
So my sunbeams can be out all day

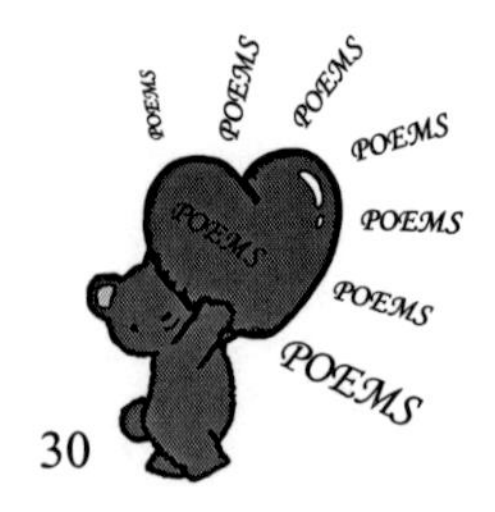

ITALIAN LADY

She came from a village of home making wine
Where oranges, lemons, grapes and olives grow divine
This lady from Italy, came to our isle
A lovely person with a cheerful smile

To settle and live with her man
Doing her best whenever she can
She was not a prisoner I am sure
Although she came after the war

Her husband now she pushes around
It's really hard work so she found
Her family for her only want the best
We all tell her she should rest

But my friend never goes too far
Not on a bus or in a car
I know she likes opera, and would go if she could
But to leave him alone, she never would

Her home is spotless and always bright
By her husband she waits day and night
His holiday they had it planned
Together they'd go to their home land

Of old times she never turned her back
And her family she never lost track
Lola is a true loyal friend
And on her one can depend

FORLORN

Standing on the corner all forlorn
Wrapped in a shawl tattered and torn
Basket of lavender she could not sell
For her the day was not going well

She tried to sell it three a penny
Most of her clients did not want any
She had no shoes on her feet
She also had very little to eat

She was mainly happy with what she had
But lately things were going bad
Her four brothers worked for the sweep
In a cold basement they would sleep

So little rent they did pay
And from the workhouse kept away
At night all would kneel and pray
Thanking the Lord for their work and play

NIGHT'S DRAW IN

As the night start to draw in
A sign of winter will soon begin
The clouds hide the summer blue sky
Even the birds are soaring high
Leaves are turning a golden brown
Even the ones that have fallen down
Hedges and grass cut to sleep
Only the ivy on the wall slowly creep
The holly is covered in lovely red berry
And her branches are getting very heavy
The old apple holds the mistletoe
It's the only place it seems to grow
The beautiful earth has changed her dress
Ready for the new spring and summer she must rest

A FREE WORLD

Across the country I love to roam
I'm a vagabond I don't need a home
In one place I could never stay
In a bed I could not lay

I sleep In the open under the stars
Away from towns ,cities smelly cars
Where the air is fresh as it can be
Everything around is beautiful and it's free

I travel when the sun brings in the light
Rest sometimes in shelter on a wet night
Earn a penny when ever I can
I'm not lazy or a begging man

I wait by the way side when I take a rest
I do most things I love the best
God gave us a free world to love and learn
This is the freedom of what I yearn

HE FOUND PEACE

The land was cracked and dry
But a willow tree began to cry
Drops like heavy falling rain
You'd think the willow was in pain

It wet my friend sitting in it's shade
But not a movement had he made
His long boat tied up by the river bank
Earlier he had filled his diesel tank

He was going fishing that night
So every thing should had to be just right
The sun was high up in the sky
A crying willow we wonder why

Did the tree know something was wrong
It stopped when my friends life was gone
He had complained of pains in his chest
For him we Could only do our best

No more tears from the willow tree
Nor his boat will we again see
His flowers floated down the river Ouse
It was his wish we could not refuse

Well dear friend you've found your peace
Fishing with the best, and at ease
God's water is beautiful and deep
The willow for you no longer does weep

CLOSE BY

When you left your earthly form
Left me alone and all forlorn
One night I saw a big new star
And I knew you were not to far

Then as I went to turn away
Your twinkling light seemed to say
Please don't turn your back
You could be on the right track

I'm here and I'm happy to stay
Misery has now gone so far away
Well dear friend your in your glory
But for me that's another story

I saw you in so much pain
I would not want you to go through that again
You were my friend and very dear
I will always know when you are near

PATIENT MAN

When he came in from the cold
He asked , am I really getting old
On his face I saw the pain
Why had I upset him again

It's along time since we met
And the longing lingers yet
If only he would sometimes phone
I hate sitting here all alone

Even the buses now he does not drive
Without him it's hard to survive
I love to see his handsome face
Feel the way he makes my heart race

We know one is to blame
We miss each other just the same
I remember places we have been
And things together we have seen

Loving words we in our hearts keep
And in our dreams when we're asleep
I love him and help him when I can
Because he is a patient man

PLEASE STAY

Sometimes I sit and wonder
If our hearts will get more fonder
Why do I have to travel alone
Why don't you ever now phone

It's you I've learnt to trust
You showed me true love not lust
Often I feel the pain
Longing for you does still remain

I know you are easy to please
And with you I feel at ease
But often my heart will cry
When you to her return why

I know you are easy caught
But it was only your house you bought
So to it you said you must return
Can't you stay, it's your love I yearn

When he holds me so tight
Everything seems so right
He really turns on the charm
Say's he is doing no one harm

How often must I always pray
That with me he might one day stay
To be apart we both get hurt
We loved each other from the start

HEARD THE CRY

The wood was still hardly a sound
Most of the animals had gone aground
The fox heard the huntsmen and their cry
He knew they would not pass him by
They'd soon pick up his scent
So away from his family he went

He was going to give them a dance
And return if he got the chance
He hated leaving his family alone
The mother would guard them whilst he was gone
His job to collect the food
Bring it to them in the wood

He had a chicken by his side
This he did his best to hide
There was a stream end of the track
He went up stream, got ready to swim back
So once again his life was spared
His family was of all he cared

MY THOUGHT'S

Once I thought I had a heart of stone
I was always on my own
You had a kind smile on your face
You simply made my heart race
I fell for you from the start
There was no cold beating in my heart
For a true love I often pray
And you walk in that summer day
With you there is nothing I lack
And I've no reason to ever look back

A BABY'S GLORY

Where dose Santa really go
There are no tracks in the snow
There are few chimneys for him to call
No fire places for presents to fall
We don't see Santa with his sack
It would be too heavy to carry on his back
Well it's the way to tell the story
Christmas is really baby Jesus' glory
We celebrate His birth
Wise men brought, incense, gold and mirth
There was a big star that night
Gave them a guiding light
In a stable all forlorn
The little baby Jesus was born
And the animals stood by
To hear the baby's first cry
But not a sound did he make
And Christmas day we don't forsake
So it's not just toys in a sack
It's a day no one will loose track

ANGLESEY ABBEY

Anglesey Abbey what a lovely treat
Better than walking around the street
No need to visit the fair or sea
You can enjoy a picnic under a tree

Just breath in the lovely fresh air
Plenty of it for all to share
A beautiful picture that has to be seen
Every shade of green ,lovely and clean

Garden with in a garden for the start
Rooms full of treasures and works of art
Shops for gifts, plants good deal
A restaurant to get a meal

It's so easy to move about
No loud radios, you don't have to shout
Even the trees whisper too
Listen to the birds and pigeons coo

Everything as nature planned
It's beautiful, God gave her a hand
There be more colour when all is out
Plenty more places if you look about

TIME FOR SPRING

Easter comes with the spring
Spring awakes nearly everything
The trees with new buds stand tall
Fresh ivy grows on the garden wall

Heather blooms over the dales
Ewes with lambs are in the vales
Chicks are now being to grow
Around the hedges young fledgling show

Everywhere starts to look it's best
A cuckoo has taken someone's nest
It was the blackbird who gave the alarm
She didn't want her babies to come to harm

So there's plenty to show spring is here
There's even signs of little deer
Things in winter that do hibernate
For the call of spring they can hardly wait

ALMOST A YEAR

You've been gone almost a year
The thought of you still brings a tear
I can no longer come to tea
And now you no longer visit me
It was a sad day when you took ill
But no one can go against God's will

So my friend of you I write
Keeping your memory in sight
You had such a lovely kind heart
And left me memories of which I'll never part
Always ready to speak your mind
A honest word, but always kind

Into the wind your ashes went
In the hills, where you're youth was spent
You're spirit no one will ever see
But I know sometimes you are close to me
We all know you were one of the best
And in God's arms now you rest

RETURNED TO GLORY

At the last supper with His followers he sat
They all had listened and enjoyed a chat
He said someone would deny him twice
Betray him when the cock crowed thrice
So when the soldiers took Our Lord away
Thirty bits of silver for him they did pay
But even today Our Lord forgives
In our hearts is where he lives
On the cross He died to save us all
Only to his father did he call
No one saw or heard Him cry
They saw the darkness of the sky
Lots of people now go to pray
On the green hill so far away
A wreath of thorns was his crown
Until the day they took him down
It was the death of the Lord Our Father's son
And amongst us now his spirit lives on
There is a lesson for us all to learn, today
God always gives his love away
From his tomb he returned to glory
In the bible you can read the full story

NATURE AWAKES

Hardly a breeze on the green hill
Even the golden daffodils are still
Slowly a bough begins to shake
As the dawn starts to break

Trees try to shake of the snow
So their buds will start to grow
And to try to keep the weather fine
A mellow sun will start to shine

The ice and snow will melt away
As the sun gets warmer every day
Winter has been cold but nice
There'll be no more skating on the ice

Even the ice must have a break
And our weight it could not take
It's to cold to take a dive
We'll wait till the earth comes alive

It has been winter and nature sleeps
And rest for the seasons she does keep
Hers is not a code to break
We wait till she tells nature to wake

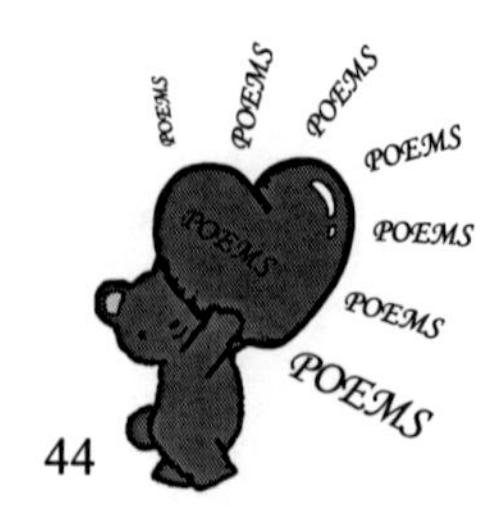

BEAUTIFUL STAR

Often as I sit I wonder why
You're so often alone and in the sky
You're always the first out at night
Shining in the heaven so bright

You're often there at the start of day
Although you're beautiful you're far away
You seem to start from the north
That's when I see you shining forth

Maybe you're the star that travelled that night
And gave the shepherds your guiding light
To tell them Mary's baby son was born
In a stable alone and forlorn

And help the three wise men with their gifts to bare
And all the people who had love to share
But beautiful star you still are bright
And still you guide so many with your light

JOY OF XMAS

Chimneys swept ready for Santa to call
We don't want the soot in his sack to fall
Stockings hanging in a colourful row
The sky looks full, it's going to snow
The room's full of fresh evergreen
Coloured lights a picture to be seen

A glass of wine, mince pie on a plate
We are hoping Santa want be late
There'll be presents under the tree
Plenty of fruit and a big turkey
Rudolf's hay is near the chimney pot
Santa's supper is keeping hot

At the door knocks the carol singers
Glad tidings sent by the bell ringers
When Santa has been we have the fire bright
Lit the room with it's flickering light
We all have a really wonderful day
From the door no one is turned away

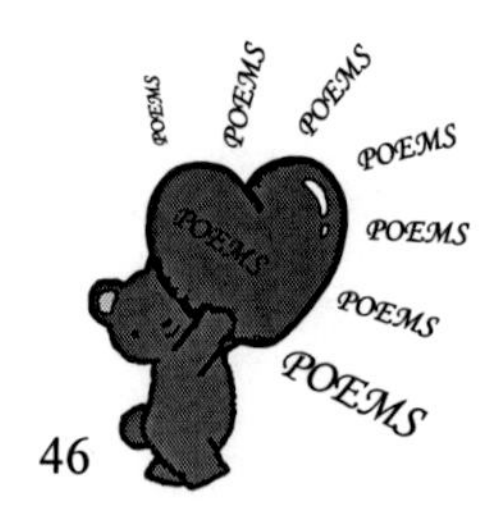

MY FAVOURITE TREE

I use to love to climb the tree
Get to the top be alone and free
I could see planes on the runway
And lots of things on a clear day

Watch the men rebuilding the steeple
And in the town lots of people
And the bombers I often saw
When they were flying off to the war

Even a crow did build her nest
High in my tree top where she could rest
But the airfield came to an end
And no more planes did we send

No more men coming to and fro
They were all de-mobbed and home did go
Now my children climb the old tree
They are happy as I use to be

Only the tree is getting old and frail
Around it they have put a rail
It has so much character and charm
Climbing it now could do it harm

SCHOOL DAYS

What's happen to hard days at school
When a dunce in the corner sat on a stool
We had to be in at the stroke of nine
Everyone quiet as we filed into line

Never tried to get in class late
That was like playing with fate
The head mistress was first to call
We had to assemble in the big hall

Our prayers daily we had to say
To the classroom we were led away
It was no fun for a beginner
To run away, you were thought a sinner

You were brought back with a clout
You'd stay in school with out a doubt
We had to change our old ways
Even parents were strict in our younger days

A cane could be very cruel
But no one could break the golden rule
If you committed a naughty sin
Instead of the cane you'd have to stay in

It was the three R's we had to learn
And any merits we had to earn
School could have been a lot of fun
When our learning days were done

WAIT AND SEE

You can't sleep when you're cold
Sometimes forget as you get old
Sometimes you sit alone and cry
And you don't always Know the reason why

Sometimes you think you look a sight
And nothing seems to turn out right
And what of the pill you forgot to take
An effort you must really make

Then you remember you have to shop
Now your of to the bus stop
It was so hot around the town
You bath and put on a gown

So now all your jobs are done
Tomorrow is bingo and some fun
After the game it's biscuits and tea
What goes on the next day wait and see

NEVER BLUE

Your more than my trusted friend
I hope our love will never end
Soon together time we must find
To let our emotions unwind

We've love each other from the start
Envious people tried to pull us apart
You taught me love and trust
Showed me true feelings not lust

To love and need you as I do
And in your arms I'm never blue
My emotions just can't fight
I wait for your return at night

My tears are not those of sorrow
I cry for the happiness of tomorrow
I know you'll always be there
And no more heartaches to bare

When you have to go away
You will always hear me say
Let my arms around you entwine
Hold your warm and tender body to mine

MEANS A LOT

Where is the land of milk and honey
All the lovely things that cost money
Money is only there to deceive
Causes a lot of worry and grief

Makes people greedy and sad
Wanting things they've never had
There are things one cannot buy
Does not matter how hard they try

We cannot buy good health
Not even if we had plenty of wealth
We can't buy trust, faith and love
These things come from God above

He gives us most things free
And shows us all the beauty to see
Be thankful what we have got
Good health and freedom means a lot

MY LOVE I GIVE

When she passes you by
How often do you want to cry
You both had to let it go
When there was no way to let you know

It's not that she wanted to hurt
You know she'd never be a flirt
You clung to you like a vine
Telling all, keep off he's mine

In our hearts we know it's not that way
My heart is yours and there to stay
So now you wait but not in vain
Your face will show me your pain

My eyes say wait for me dear heart
Your love is what I am a part
To you all my love I will give
It's all yours as long as live

NEEDS TO BE

There were times he could not bare
When she was not with him to share
His thought he had to hide
He longed for her by his side

Her photo he always carried it around
It gave him peace so he found
And at her photo he would glance
He'd be by her side if he got the chance

She still held the chain to his heart
It was a shame they were apart
He worked hard and he did pray
That sometime they would find a way

Being together was no disgrace
He loved to see her lovely face
For her family he wanted to care
And all the things they could share

EARLY MORNING

With early morning comes the dew
Everything ready to start anew
Nearly all the birds have built a nest
And the ground was ploughed to rest
Falling leaves covered the cooling ground
There is acorns that a squirrel has found
She has forgotten where she stored her hoard
Leaking sacks where rats and mice have gnawed
The hay for the horses is nicely stacked
The seed is sorted and freshly packed
There is hardly any rest on the farm
Everything checked so nothing comes to harm
Thank God for His helping hand
Now all is ready to reset the land

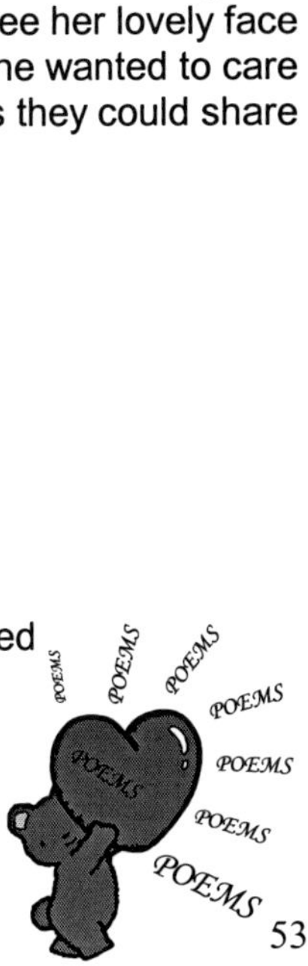

CROMWELL

As a land owner he was on the right track
But as a soldier, he never once looked back
But first at school he did very well
He was known as Oliver Cromwell
His family had land and wealth
As far as we know he was in good health
But local administration he had a part to play
And with the parliamentary army he did stay
Commanding his own cavalry regiment
Against the royalist he was sent
Nothing this roundhead would not tackle
Successful in all sieges and battle
His army played a major role in parliamentary victory
The battle was sealed in June 1645 he won at Nasby
Civil war flared again, and the royalists fled
After his trial the royalist king lost his head
Cromwell attributed his success to Gods will
Historians point to his courage and skill
His care in training and equipping his men
And his strict discipline over the fen
He became Lord Protector an important key
He brought peace in the troubled period of British history

ENTWINE

Your more than a true friend
Our love we know will never end
I've tried to put how I feel to rhyme
Be together if we had more time

Though lately we are often apart
But we fell for each other from the start
You taught me trust, love so true
I'm no longer lonely or blue

My emotions I can't get right
Although I wait for you each night
I pray for another tomorrow
My tears are not ones for sorrow

You try to protect me from harm
Making me feel happy and calm
So by your side, I want to stay
Hoping dear God will show us the way

OFF THE LINE

An angler went fishing on his bike
To catch himself a nice big pike
Everything was going fine
There was a pull on his line

Oh my, by gee, oh golly
He's gone and caught a shopping trolley
After chasing off a coot
More fun he caught a boot

Then got hooked into an old sack
He would not put that rubbish back
Then to his rod he had to rush
He landed his pike in a bush

Then things went from bad to worse
When catching the reeds he did curse
Fed up with dredging the river bed
He went home to watch TV, instead

WHO WANTED MORE

Mum took the soldiers washing in
They brought the powder in a big tin
All by hand we did the ironing and scrubbing
No machine to do any of the washing
We order ones had to do some jobs
Fetching coal and getting logs
Go to the garden for the veg
If fine trim the hedge
Some things were needed every day
If work was short dad could not pay
So clothing coupons help with the rent
Sweet coupons to an aunt was sent
In return she sent us jam and meat
Things she never herself would eat
Dad always mended the shoes we wore
We had to mend the clothes we tore
Rags were cut to peg a mat
Un-picked old jumpers for socks or a hat
Second hand, or hand me down clothes to wear
Washed, altered, to refuse we would not dare
This is how we lived in the years of war
Happy, poorly shod, loved, who could ask for more

WHAT PEOPLE BELIEVED

Moses start was not very good
The king would have slain him if he could
The wicked man had all baby sons killed
And thought his wish had been full filled
But Moses mother hid him in the reeds
He was found brought up to do his good deeds

Not in the shadows did he walk
And to the people he would talk
The Lord told Moses to take his people away
And Moses for the Lord did obey
At the river the Lord helped them to cross
And at that time no one was loss

So as people ventured to places new
God told Moses what He wanted him to do
In the mountains alone Moses would pray
The ten commandments he brought back that day
Moses told his people, this is God's law and word
Every day in a sermon, that's what the people heard

COULD IT BE PEACE

Now in the sky the stars are bright
As they were a long time ago on a similar night
Some seem to fade or decline
But now they looked so devine
The shepherds were the first to see a change
An angel appeared as it came into range

Please don't be afraid of my light
I've come to tell you what happened to night
In a stable not so far away
Our baby Jesus was born today
First gifts were brought by three wise men
We have celebrated his birth since then

Sometimes we see the friendly star
It does not always travel that far
When the moon is so bright
We can see them clearly burning bright
But no angels now do we see
They say peace on earth as it was meant to be

CHRISTMAS MADNESS

All things are not what they seem
Even you may chase a moonbeam
The fairy doll has laddered her tights
The cat has switch off the lights
The fairies wand has started to sag
Santa forgot where he put his bag
The tree has shed it's needles on the floor
Someone went out and slammed the door
What a way for Santa to call
Mother shouting in the hall
So his dad had packed and moved away
Because of the shouting he would not stay
To make the boy happy no one was trying
He stopped in his room, he was crying
Was this the Christmas his parents planned
Just something he did not understand

TREES

Holly in her coat of dark evergreen
With her red berries is the winter queen
The mistletoe is also a lovely bush
But her berries you can easy crush
Some yew trees play a part
Pleases all the young at heart
Now other trees and bushes are bare
The winter greenery they don't share
A Christmas rose blooms by the wall
Waiting for the first snow to fall
Evergreens cut to decorate inside
Across the sky Santa will ride
It's the time of year we all keep
Whilst the children are fast asleep
God made nature to grow this way
To help to keep our Lord's day

ON THE GO

He never carries his little black case
But around the hospital he goes in haste
He had a lot of people to see
So there was no time for coffee or tea
He does not have time to dine
Do personal things he doesn't have time
He has not enough hours in a day
So on his feet he has to stay
Does not get time for a meal
The house surgeon has a very rough deal
He never flies up the wall
Always ready to take that call
In his white coat and stethoscope
Always there to give us hope
You moan when he wont let you out
But he knows what it's all about
He loves to see you walk away
When in the ward you had to stay

WHAT I SEE

Out side my window is a tree
In the summer the birds I can see
Some already built their nest
Very high away from the pest
He's not a very friendly cat
And a little bird he'd soon have that
Sometimes the fledglings will fall
And in vain one of the parents will call
To fall was the babies fate
Sadly the alarm was too late
And the mother fluttered around
The baby was never found

HE MADE US WELCOME

The bells said time to come in
People were getting ready to sing
The reader made us welcome
His sermon ready to be done
The first hymn was of love
Praises sent to our Father above

The psalm was one I never knew
So I stood quietly in my pew
His prayers was a lovely choice
Made people happy and rejoice
The whole sermon pulled at the heart
The story held us from the start

The complete service gave us warmth
The peoples attention he gather forth
He really chose the right word
You could visualise what you heard
He was so good to hear and see
A vicar is what he really should be

SNOWDROPS

Why do you wait for spring to grow
In the shade mostly covered in snow
One of the first to show your head
In the woods or a flower bed
Boldly you break up the gloom
With your lovely delicate bloom
You never hold your face to the light
Maybe for you the winter sun is to bright
As soon as we see you appear
We know that spring is nearly here
Slowly as other flowers bloom near by
You disappear I wonder why
With the snow you seem to go
Maybe that's what makes you grow

KINGFISHER

When the kingfisher pays her call
To the river, lake or waterfall
In the sandy banks, she'll build her nest
A place she finds the very best
Just a small hole left in the bank
Not far from where a old boat sank
In the river she will dive for small fry
Or to catch insects and moths as they go by
They never go straight to the nest
This way they keep away the pest
In the bank the little ones cry
You can hear them as you pass by
The kingfisher is a colourful bird
But it's call hardly anyone has heard
Keeps their nest out of sight
The babies come out when the time is right
Near the water they sat till they heard a call
They're happy and safe near the waterfall

A BAND OF GOLD

When love comes from cupids arrow
Some brings joy for tomorrow
To our heart cupid paid his call
My tears ran like a water fall

Cupid's gold arrow brought us together
My trust, love and faith, we hold for the better
There's times we have to be apart
That does not mean a broken heart

Although I'd rather stay with you
It's something we have to do
Together our love we did seal
Being apart seems unreal

Down memory lane we often walk
But one day we wont just sit and talk
Cupids arrow is the band of gold
But the love story may never be told

MY KIDS

Our names are Jenny and Jane
Being cats our names are plain
In the window we look out
To see who or what is about
We never go out in the cold
Always do as we are told
Plenty of biscuits and meat
Even get fresh fish for a treat
Our toys are on the floor
We never go out of the door
We have a tray to do our job
We're not allowed with the mob
Not allowed to dig in a garden
The flat is our place, with our guardian

BIG HITS

It's so crowded in the town
Not one place you can sit down
Shops are packed and the street
All you get is tired aching feet

People needing a fag or fresh air
Stand about and at you glare
It looks as if you taken up the room
And it's a miserable day full of gloom

Well at last the sun came out
The children started to shout
But you're so very up tight
Nothing up to now as come out right

No good making a fuss
Might as well go on the next bus
Well thank God for that cup of tea
DID you enjoy that trip with me

MIGRATE

Across the sky the clouds to race
Leaving the moon to show his face
The sun lightened up the day
keeping the cold winds at bay

The evenings now are very cold
Falling leaves turn to gold
The rain hardly gave us a break
The river took all it could take

Most birds have now migrated
To travel afar where they are fated
We can see the star at night
Maybe tomorrow all will be bright

SEASONS CHANGE

When squirrels, dormice, hedgehogs go to sleep
It's winter and their food they hid to keep
But even winter has to survive
Even when our world does not seem alive
A hungry fox is on the prowl
So is the screeching old owl

Pigeons pulling rape up by the root
So these pest the farmer will shoot
In winters cover a lot will sleep
As it gets warmer out all will creep
Nature shows the world is full of colour
And who could find a better cover

SPRING

Strong winds cause the leafs to fall
Heaping them up by the garden wall
Or leave them untidy on the ground
And berries and nuts can be found

Or put into a compost heap to lay
To be used when they have gone to decay
Into hedge bottoms some did go
To get cover by the frost and snow

Only the holly and yew stand proud
They are green all year round
Evergreens could be an Xmas tree
Decorated for all to see

Lots of seeds the wind will take
To give the earth another break
Snow comes, the robin will sing
And we know it's time for spring

PONY EXPRESS

Children can't walk on me can ride
With someone walking by my side
Children who can't talk; me they can touch
I love little children so very much

Children that are blind ,can trust me
I've only one eye, but still can see
I can move with speed and grace
With children I go at a slow pace

Once I use to jump poles
Now I only jump small holes
I'm a beast for a mint or carrot
But they make me repeat like a parrot

I never ever get the hump
I do enjoy a sugar lump
An apple they will try to hide
I smell it giving the children a ride

I know the lady will give it to me
She always brings me titbits for tea
Children, already for the pony express
Riding with the disabled is the best

BIRDS

Did you hear the cuckoo call
See the robin in the ivy on the wall
Hear the jackdaw, he's a pest
With the magpie will rob a nest

Hear the rooks and crows in a tree
The starlings starting to disagree
The blackbird for some reason is cross
Trying to show a thrush she's the boss

Swallows, martins, build in the eaves
Protecting their eggs from the thieves
Pigeons and doves coo from the park
Owls hoot after it's dark

Pheasants fly off giving a warning
A coot and moorhen to mates are calling
Come autumn a lot will migrate
They seem to know and never late

TO DREAM

When you sail across the sea
Do you often remember me
I was the one who always loss
You thought you could be the boss

But now I often sit and cry
No one ever asked me why
Why the one I loved move away
Yes I really regret that day

Not many places have I seen
Often of places I will dream
Now I work so I can pay
For a holiday far away

I dream of going to Switzerland
On a sleigh across the icy land
Travelling over the lovely snow
Will I do only the Lord does know

A LOVING FEELING

When your near me though the night
And our feelings know all is right
And come the dawn you have to go
But the reason only we both know

Now I have won your loving tender heart
There is no one who can make us part
Two hearts entwined by a lovers chain
With the Lord's help that's how they will remain

WHEN WINTER COMES

Snow lay thickly on the ground
Birds searching for what can be found
Children building in the snow
Cold hands and noses aglow

Down the hill they will slide
With a small one by their side
Weathering another snow storm
Wrapped up to keep themselves warm

Pine logs throw out heat into the room
At night curtains will keep out the gloom
But not every one has heat
Or warm clothing or shoes on their feet

Some around the country roam
They don't even have a home
The evening prayer will soon begin
For a warm the church they could go in

No one is ever turned away
Allis welcome every Sunday
It's time for us all to pray
Thank the Lord for granting us the day

Ask Him to bless the food we eat
And for any special treats
Ask Him to stop countries at war
And help the people who are now poor

WE LOOKED

Just how life could really be
And the things we don't want to see
Some time in life we take a look
Like reading the chapters from a book
There is often a good story to tell
A broken romance not going too well
A lot of things that went stale
Like telling half a story, part of a tale
A lot you know by heart
How often did you play the part
How life has so many a reason
Love and trust through a difficult season
You can close a book today
But memories you put away
Thinking of what may come tomorrow
Could be happiness, or sorrow
We can do in life mostly anything
And be thankful for what life does bring

TIME TO THINK

To every year there is a season
We don't really know the reason
We don't lose the human side of things
No matter how mechanised our would brings
Remember the days rushing through the town
Now is the time to rest ,and settle down
Through the years you pass on your skill
Now is the time your wishes you should fill
Knowing every day is for living
The precious memories you are giving
No one can live in the past
Yesterday has gone, the future will last
Make an effort and be bright
God helps everything to turn out right

A FRIEND WE NEED

The Lord is a friend we'll always need
He teaches us how to do our good deed
So now as I try to write, and pray
I don't always no what to say
Please help our reader a loyal man
He always does the best he can
Please help our children everyday
So they wont go a far or stray

Help us to show them life is real
Honesty pays, you should never steal
And dear Lord our soul to keep
When we settle down to sleep
Help all to thank for our daily bread
Stick to the commandments as the bible said
Help us though our grief and pain
When we feel life is a stain

Thank you for the light at night
When the moon is shining bright
When we travel late in the day
Your bright star shows us the way
Thank you for the good things we eat
And the friendly faces that we meet
Thank you for giving us our church reader
He shows us the friend we need, he is a true believer

A MILLENNIUM ROSE

The garden was so beautifully planned
With mother nature giving a helping hand
For the millennium we planted a rose
We will watch how lovely it grows

We set seedlings in a frame of glass
Letting the frost and cold winds pass
Aromatic herbs on the window sill
When dried little pots we can fill

Hanging basket another rose around the door
More miniature roses on the patio floor
From the garden the choice is wide
All the beauty we can see from inside

RINGING TRUE

The look that came into your eyes
Took my feeling by surprise
Words, I wanted I thought you'd never tell
Did my love for you break the spell

You say your love belongs to no other
You do not need another lover
There's only one way it can be
I'll wait for the day you come to me

You say I'm more than a friend
We're together all the time we can spend
I found a loyal man in you
Now things are starting to ring true

You understand my funny ways
Making me happy every day
No truer lover can I find
You always give me peace of mind

ALL CHANGE

How quickly does the weather change
Days get shorter it seems so strange
The wind blows hard and cold
Must be a sign I'm getting old

Once I played in deep snow
Oh, where did my childhood go
Times I still try to memorise
Now looking back I realise

We use to play long hours in the dark
In the fields ,by the lamp in the park
Even the snow don't come that deep
Covering the ground so the earth could sleep

You no longer hear children out at night
They watch TV, in a blazing light
They hardly go walking in the sun
Computers have taken over their fun

Food from freezers, tins or a jar
Never walk, go out in the family car
Oh, am I just making a fuss
I walk, if it rains get a bus

POEMS
POEMS
POEMS
POEMS
POEMS
POEMS
POEMS
POEMS

INDEX

A BABY'S GLORY 39
A BAND OF GOLD 64
A FREE WORLD 33
A FRIEND WE NEED 72
A LOVING FEELING 69
A MILLENNIUM ROSE 73
A NANNA'S SMILE 15
ALL CHANGE 74
ALMOST A YEAR 42
ANGLESEY ABBEY 40

BEAUTIFUL STAR 45
BEDTIME STORY 27
BEING A JERK 11
BIG HITS 65
BIRDS 68

CHRISTMAS MADNESS 60
CLOSE BY 35
COLD NIGHT 14
COULD IT BE PEACE 59
CROMWELL 54

DAY DREAMER 26
DAYS OF OLD 10

EARLY MORNING 53
ENTWINE 55

FORLORN 32

HE FOUND PEACE 34
HE FOUND THE BEST 24
HE LOVES US 19
HE MADE US WELCOME 62
HEARD THE CRY 38

IF ONLY 21
IN STYLE 5
ITALIAN LADY 31

JOY OF XMAS 46

KINGFISHER 63

LIGHT OF WAY 8
LITTLE LADY 20
LITTLE OLD LADY 12

MEANS A LOT 51
MIGRATE 65
MY FAVOURITE TREE 47
MY KIDS 64
MY LOVE I GIVE 52
MY THOUGHT'S 38

NATURE AWAKES 44
NEEDS TO BE 53
NEVER BE AFRAID 7
NEVER BLUE 50
NEVER DULL 25
NIGHT'S DRAW IN 33

OFF THE LINE 56
ON THE GO 61
OUR SPECIAL LADY 18

PATIENT MAN 36
PLEASE STAY 37
PONY EXPRESS 67

RETURNED TO GLORY 43
RHYME AND LAUGH 13
RINGING TRUE 73

SEASONS CHANGE 66
SCHOOL DAYS 48
SEARCHING 9
SHADOWS 9
SNOWDROPS 63
SPRING 66
SPRING BEAUTY 19
SUNBEAMS 30

TENDERNESS 8
THE PASSING YEARS 6
THE PHOTOGRAPH 16
THE SHEPHERD 22
THEY WAKE WITH THE DAWN 29
TIME FOR SPRING 41
TIME TO THINK 71
TO DREAM 69
TO LEARN THE TRUTH 17
TREES 60

VERY RELUCTANT TO GO 28

WAIT AND SEE 49
WE HAVE CHANGED 23
WE LOOKED 71
WHAT PEOPLE BELIEVED 58
WHAT TO SEE 61
WHEN WINTER COMES 70
WHERE I REST 25
WHO WANTED MORE 57
WHY 11